It Started with Pizza

Variables, Expressions, and Equations

Dawn McMillan

Publishing Credits

Editor
Sara Johnson

Editorial Director
Dona Herweck Rice

Editor-in-Chief
Sharon Coan, M.S.Ed.

Creative Director
Lee Aucoin

Publisher
Rachelle Cracchiolo, M.S.Ed.

Image Credits

The authors and publisher would like to gratefully credit or acknowledge the following for permission to reproduce copyright material: cover Pearson Education/Lindsay Edwards; p.1 Pearson Education/Lindsay Edwards; p.3 Pearson Education/Lindsay Edwards; p.4 Alamy; p.5 Pearson Education/Lindsay Edwards: p.6 Pearson Education/Lindsay Edwards; p.7 Big Stock Photo; p.8 Big Stock Photo; p.9 Dreamstime; p.11 Corbis; p.12 Shutterstock; p.13 (top) Big Stock Photo; p.13 (bottom) Rob Cruse; p.14 (top left) Shutterstock; p.14 (top middle) 123 Royalty-Free; p. 14 (top right) Pearson Education/Alice McBroom; 14 (bottom left) iStock Photo; p.14 (bottom middle) Shutterstock; p.14 (bottom right) iStock Photo; p.16 Shutterstock; p.17 Photos.com; p.18 123 Royalty-Free; p.19 Shutterstock; pp.20-21 Photolibrary.com/Detlev Van Ravenswaay; 22 (left) Photolibrary.com/Gerard Fritz; p.22 (right) Big Stock Photo; p.23 (both) Big Stock Photo; p.24 NASA; p.26 (all) Big Stock Photo; p.27 iStock; p.29 Shutterstock

While every care has been taken to trace and acknowledge copyright, the publishers tender their apologies for any accidental infringement where copyright has proved untraceable. They would be pleased to come to a suitable arrangement with the rightful owner in each case.

Teacher Created Materials

5301 Oceanus Drive
Huntington Beach, CA 92649-1030
http://www.tcmpub.com

ISBN 978-0-7439-0911-2

Table of
Contents

Math in Food

On my birthday, I invited two of my friends to a pizza restaurant for dinner. Of course, we ordered pizza. We all love pizza! We sat with Mom and Dad, and my older brother. The waiter brought two pizzas to the table.

"Two pizzas!" joked Dad. "One for Mom and me to eat, and one for the rest of you!"

"That is unfair!" I exclaimed. "That means that you and Mom will have 2 slices each, which is half of the pizza. We will only have 1 slice each. That is only one quarter of the pizza!"

"Never mind!" said Mom. "We can order another pizza. The four of you can share 2 pizzas."

Before we knew it, the waiter had delivered another pizza for us kids to share.

"So," said my older brother, who thinks he is really good at math, "if we all eat a quarter from both of the pizzas, what fraction of a whole pizza will each of us eat?"

Our pizzas

LET'S EXPLORE MATH

Variables (VAIR-ee-uh-buhls) are letters or symbols that can be used to **represent** numbers. Often, the letter x is used to represent a number. An **equation** is a mathematical sentence that shows 2 equal numbers or quantities. It is written with an equal sign.

Look at the pictures above. They show the pizzas that were eaten at the birthday dinner. Each pizza had 4 slices. The equation $\frac{1}{4} + \frac{1}{4} = x$ can be used to find what fraction of the pizza each kid ate.

a. What does x represent?

b. What does x equal?

I looked at my two friends. "Easy!" I said. "We each eat a quarter from one pizza, then a quarter from the other. That makes two quarters, which makes half a pizza. We will each be eating the same fraction of pizza as Mom and Dad! We could write an equation to show the equivalent fractions: $\frac{2}{4} = \frac{1}{2}$."

$$\frac{2}{4} = \frac{1}{2}$$

We each ate 2 quarters of pizza.

Mom and Dad each ate half a pizza.

Later that night, back at home, I grabbed an apple for a snack. I cut the apple into slices. Quickly, my older brother ate 3 of the slices. There were 5 slices left for me. I used math to figure out how many slices I started with.

How Many Slices?

I can use the equation $x - 3 = 5$ to figure out how many slices I started with.
x represents the number of slices I started with.
3 represents the number of slices my brother ate.
5 represents the number of slices I had left.

I can add to solve for x.
$x - 3 = 5$
$5 + 3 = x$
$5 + 3 = 8$
That means I started with 8 slices.

Math Is Everywhere

My brother and I talked more about math later that night. We realized that we could use math to figure out how many hours we sleep each school night. Our bedtime is 8:00 P.M. and we wake up at 7:00 A.M. in order to get ready for school.

These clocks show what time we get up and what time we go to bed.

7:00 A.M.   8:00 P.M.

As my head hit the pillow, I was still thinking about math. I thought about the **environment** and the world around me. I thought about all the things that people do. And I began to understand that math is everywhere.

I decided that tomorrow I would do a test to see how many places I could find math throughout the day.

LET'S EXPLORE MATH

An **expression** is a group of variables, numbers, and operations that stand for a number or quantity. An expression does not have an equal sign.

The next day, I counted the vehicles we passed on the road during the drive to school. I counted 25 cars, 14 SUVs, and some buses. I realized I could write an expression to show the total number of vehicles we passed.

Write the expression discussed above.

Math at Home

In the Bedroom

After school, I looked around my bedroom for different examples of math. Each thing in my room takes up a different amount of space.

So I used grid paper and made a simple floor plan of my room. I sketched how much space my bed takes up. I also have a desk, a bookcase, a dresser, a night stand, and a rug. My brother helped me work out how much space each piece of furniture takes up.

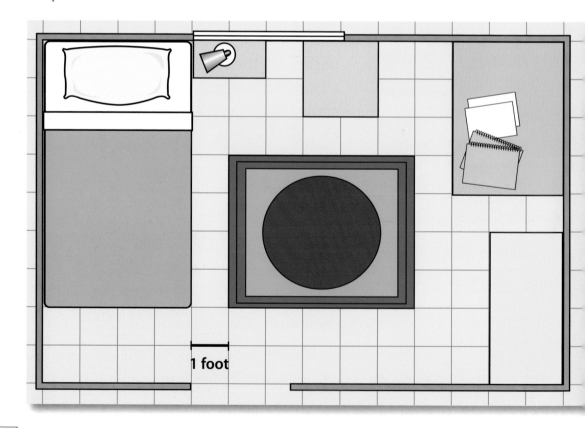

1 foot

I realized that math could be shown in my floor plan. I could calculate the perimeters and areas of all of the objects in my room. I could also use the **dimensions** to rearrange my room and design a new floor plan.

LET'S EXPLORE MATH

The total area of the bedroom is 126 square feet. The bedroom furniture takes up 74 square feet. Let x represent the amount of unused space in the bedroom.

a. What equation could be used to find the amount of unused space in the room?

b. Solve the equation you wrote in problem **a**.

c. What would you do with the unused space?

In the Kitchen

Then I went into the kitchen to help make dinner. The kitchen is another great room for finding math. **Recipes** show measurements of ingredients. And recipe sizes can be increased or decreased using multiplication and division.

Mom's Pizza Dough
Makes 1 pizza crust

Ingredients

2 cups plain flour
$\frac{3}{4}$ cup warm water
1 teaspoon super fine sugar
$\frac{1}{2}$ teaspoon salt
2 tablespoons olive oil
8 grams of dry yeast

There are many kitchen tools that are used to measure ingredients. Measuring spoons are different sizes: $\frac{1}{8}$ teaspoon, $\frac{1}{2}$ teaspoon, and $\frac{1}{4}$ teaspoon. They are all fractions of 1 teaspoon. Measuring cups are marked with fractional measurements: $\frac{1}{2}$ cup, $\frac{1}{3}$ cup, and $\frac{1}{4}$ cup. They are all fractions of 1 cup.

measuring spoons

measuring cups

$\frac{1}{3}$ cup

$\frac{1}{4}$ cup

1 cup

$\frac{1}{2}$ cup

13

Mom and I decide to make pizza for dinner. We follow her recipe, but we have to double it to make 2 pizzas. To do this, we multiply each **quantity** in the recipe by 2.

It was easy to double the quantities of the flour, sugar, olive oil, and dry yeast. The fractions made it harder to double the amount of water and salt. Mom suggested using repeated addition instead.

Double Quantities

Water
$$\frac{3}{4} + \frac{3}{4} = \frac{6}{4} = 1\frac{1}{2} \text{ cups warm water}$$

Salt
$$\frac{1}{2} + \frac{1}{2} = \frac{2}{2} = 1 \text{ teaspoon salt}$$

dry yeast

water

salt

olive oil

flour

super fine sugar

Mathematical Names

As Mom and I were cooking, I realized that we can talk about numbers in different ways. I looked at our kitchen scale. Two cups of flour weighs about 8 ounces. If 8 ounces equals $\frac{1}{2}$ pound, then 8 ounces is also 50% of a pound. And 50% can also be written as a decimal number, 0.5.

The quantity remains the same. It does not matter if you use the decimal, percentage, or fractional name.

LET'S EXPLORE MATH

When we doubled the pizza-dough recipe, we calculated that we needed 16 grams of dry yeast. Dry yeast comes in packets that hold 2 grams each. We can use the variable p to represent the number of packets we need to use.

a. Which equation below could be used to find the number of packets needed for the recipe?

1. $2 + p = 16$ **2.** $2p = 16$ **3.** $2 \div p = 16$

b. Use the equation you chose to figure out how many packets of yeast are needed for the recipe.

Math and the Human Body

Dad came into the kitchen. "I will show you something else to do with math," he said. "Come with me!"

He led me to a full-length mirror. Then he stood in front of it. "A great example of **proportions** stares out at us from the mirror!" he said.

I looked at Dad's **reflection**. His head takes up about $\frac{1}{8}$ of his body. So, the human body stands about 8 heads high. That means a body is about as tall as 8 heads of that body, stacked on top of each other.

In other words, the ratio of the head to the whole body is 1 to 8; the head is $\frac{1}{8}$ of the height of the whole body.

Then Dad stepped away from the mirror. "Now it is your turn," he told me. "Look closely at your face."

I looked at my reflection. I noticed that my face was **symmetrical**.

Next, I found a magazine. I looked at some faces and saw how they were symmetrical, too.

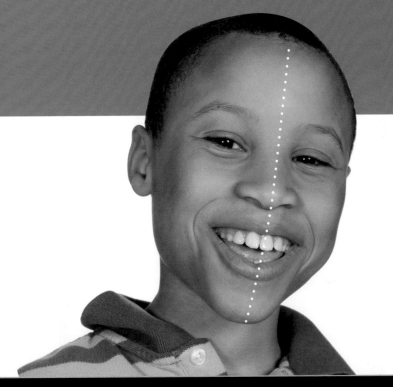

More Faces

There were 4 faces in the magazine that were not symmetrical. Those people had freckles. I wrote an expression to show the total number of faces I found in the magazine: 4 + 18.
What does the number 18 represent?

18 represents the number of people with symmetrical faces.

After dinner, I went outside to play with my neighborhood friends. I noticed my friend's younger sister, Nita, had some adult teeth growing in. She told me that she has 7 adult teeth. Altogether, she has 20 teeth. I can use the variable t to figure out how many baby teeth she has left.

How Many Teeth?

$7 + t = 20$

$20 - 7 = t$

$20 - 7 = 13$

Nita has 13 baby teeth left!

LET'S EXPLORE MATH

While playing, a group of my neighborhood friends are discussing how tall they are. Luis is 55 inches tall, Madeleine is 56 inches tall, and Jamie does not know her height.

a. Write an expression to show the combined height of all three friends.

The total combined height for all 3 friends is 162 inches:
$55 + 56 + x = 162$

b. What is Jamie's height?

c. Who is the tallest?

Math in Space

When I came in from playing, Mom came into my room to see what I was doing.

"What about math in space?" asked Mom. "Think about the size of the planets in our **solar system**. Maybe we could make a proportional model of some of the planets."

The planets that make up our solar system

Mom told me that **astronomers** collect proportional data about the solar system. Our solar system is huge in size and distance. There are 8 planets and a sun in our solar system. Some of the planets are smaller than Earth. Some are much larger.

LET'S EXPLORE MATH

There are 8 planets in our solar system. Mercury, Venus, Earth, and Mars are called *inner planets*. The rest of the planets are called *outer planets*.

a. Write an equation to show the number of outer planets.

b. How many outer planets are in our solar system?

Dad suggested that we **research** the size of the planets and the sun on the Internet. It was amazing. I had not realized just how large the solar system is, or how big some of the planets are. The sun is a star. It is even bigger than all the planets in our solar system combined!

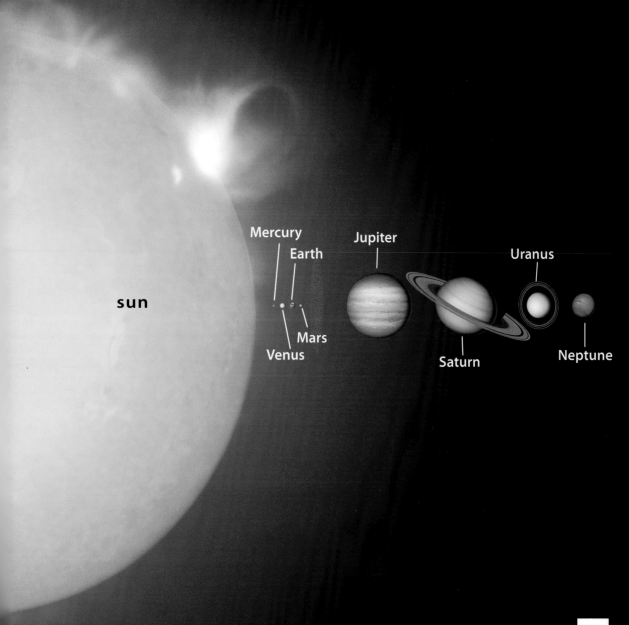

sun

Mercury

Earth

Mars

Venus

Jupiter

Saturn

Uranus

Neptune

The more I thought about the solar system, the harder it was to **visualize** the size of the planets in it. So Mom helped me some more.

First, we found out the actual **diameter** of the sun and the planets. Mom got me to write them down. Then, Mom helped me change the diameter of the planets from kilometers into millimeters! Then Mom reduced that number by 100 million. So, our scale is 1 millimeter = 1,000 kilometers.

sun = giant pumpkin

It was a lot of hard work. Mom used her calculator to help her. But it was worth it. Mom and I found a great way to make a proportional model of the planets and the sun using food.

The proportional model helped me see just how big the sun is compared to Earth. It was amazing!

Star/Planet	Actual Diameter (km)	Reduced Diameter (mm)	Food Items (in approximate proportional size)
sun (a star)	1,391,980	1,392	giant pumpkin
Mercury	4,900	4.9	coffee bean
Venus	12,100	12.1	large blueberry
Earth	12,700	12.7	cherry
Mars	6,700	6.7	pea
Jupiter	142,000	142	large grapefruit or cantaloupe
Saturn	120,000	120	very large orange
Uranus	51,800	51.8	kiwi
Neptune	49,500	49.5	apricot or nectarine

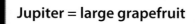
Jupiter = large grapefruit

Earth = cherry

"Now imagine trying to work out proportional distances for our solar system," said Mom.

That made me stop and think some more. During my Internet research on planet sizes, I had found the distance of each planet from the sun. I had read on the Internet that Earth is over 92 million miles (over 148 million km) from the sun. And Jupiter is around 484 million miles (779 million km) from the sun.

LET'S EXPLORE MATH

Only 6 of the 8 planets in our solar system have moons. Saturn has 60 moons. Jupiter has 3 more moons than Saturn. Write an equation to show how many moons Jupiter has.

The table below shows the distance of each planet from the sun. The distances in our solar system are really incredible!

Planet Distances from the Sun

Planet	Distance	
	Miles	Kilometers
Inner Planets		
Mercury	35,983,093	57,909,175
Venus	67,237,912	108,208,930
Earth	92,955,819	149,597,890
Mars	141,633,262	227,936,640
Outer Planets		
Jupiter	483,682,805	778,412,020
Saturn	886,526,063	1,426,725,400
Uranus	1,783,939,419	2,870,972,200
Neptune	2,795,084,767	4,498,252,899

That's Far!

I can use variables and expressions to show planets' distances from the sun. Mars is about 4 times farther away from the sun than Mercury. The variable m can represent the distance Mercury is from the sun. So, the expression $4m$ can represent the distance Mars is from the sun.

Let's say my house was Earth, or the cherry. Then the sun, or giant pumpkin, would need to be about a city block away. And Jupiter, or the large grapefruit, would have to be about five blocks away from the pumpkin.

sun

1 city block

Earth

5 city blocks

Jupiter

A proportional model of the distances in the solar system would not fit in my house!

Math Gives Meaning

My brain was buzzing. In just one day, I learned so much about math in the world around me. I love thinking about math. It makes my world so much more interesting. It's amazing to think that I learned so much, and it all started from eating pizza!

Space Discovery

Astronomers have just discovered a new solar system in a distant galaxy. It has six planets orbiting around a sun. Some of the planets are about the size of Earth. Others are much larger. And this new solar system has a combined total of 30 moons!

The table below is missing some of the current information astronomers have learned about this new solar system.

Planets in New Solar System

Name of Planet	Approximate Diameter (miles)	Number of Moons
Zenner	z	1
Xenox	3,000	x
Axiom	a	2
Centaur	75,000	c
Yukka	36,000	17

Solve It!

For each question below, write mathematical equations using variables to help you figure out the answers.

a. Xenox has 15 fewer moons than Yukka. How many moons does Xenox have?

b. Centaur has 6 more moons than Axiom. How many moons does Centaur have?

Centaur's diameter is 68,500 miles bigger than Zenner's diameter. Axiom's diameter and Xenox's diameter total 4,000 miles.

c. What are the diameters of planets Zenner and Axiom?

Use the steps below to help you solve the problems above.

Step 1: Use the information in the table to write question **a.** as a mathematical equation. Then solve your equation.

Step 2: Use the information in the table to write question **b.** as a mathematical equation. Then solve your equation.

Step 3: Use the information in the table and above question **c.** to write mathematical equations. Then solve your equations.

Glossary

astronomers—people who study objects and matter outside the Earth's atmosphere

diameter—a line joining 2 points of a circle and passing through its center

dimensions—the measurements of shapes; 2-D objects have width and length

environment—the place in which people and other animals live, and the circumstances under which they live

equation—a mathematical sentence that shows 2 equal numbers or quantities; written with an equal sign

expression—a group of symbols or numbers standing for a number or quantity; a mathematical phrase without an equal sign

proportions—a statement that ratios are equal; $\frac{4}{8} = \frac{1}{2}$

quantity—the amount or number of something

recipes—instructions for cooking food

reflection—a mirror image of something

represent—stand in place of; to stand for

research—to study and investigate something

solar system—the part in space that is made up of all the planets that orbit the sun, including moons, comets, asteroids, and meteoroids

symmetrical—having balance in size, shape, and position on opposite sides of a dividing line

variables—symbols or letters representing unknown values

visualize—to see or form a picture of something in your mind

Index

Let's Explore Math

Page 5:

a. x represents the fraction of a pizza each child ate

b. x equals $\frac{2}{4}$ or $\frac{1}{2}$ of a pizza

Page 9:

$25 + 14 + x$

Page 11:

a. $126 - 74 = x$

b. 52 square feet (ft.^{2})

c. Answers will vary.

Page 15:

a. **2.** $2p = 16$

b. 8 packets

Page 18:

a. $55 + 56 + x$

b. Jamie's height is 51 inches.

c. Madeleine is the tallest.

Page 20:

a. $4 + x = 8$

b. 4 planets

Page 24:

$60 + 3 = x$

Problem-Solving Activity

a. $17 - 15 = x$

$17 - 15 = 2$ moons

Xenox has 2 moons.

b. $2 + 6 = c$

$2 + 6 = 8$ moons

Centaur has 8 moons.

c. $75,000 - 68,500 = z$

$75,000 - 68,500 = 6,500$ miles in diameter

Zenner has a diameter of 6,500 miles.

$3,000 + a = 4,000$

$4,000 - 3,000 = a$

$4,000 - 3,000 = 1,000$ miles in diameter

Axiom has a diameter of 1,000 miles.